To the *Pointe* WORKBOOK

Carol Reeder

ISBN-13: 978-1-937458-89-8

Printed in the United States of America.

PREPARING

For Your Assessments

Pre-Pointe ASSESSMENTS

#1 Standing Posture in 1st
aligned, turned out with shoulder blades flat

#2 Demi-Plié Alignment in 5th
aligned as in #1 with knees over toes in plié

#3 Demi-Plié Depth - Right
the ability to plié 2 1/2" to 4 1/2"

#4 Demi-Plié Depth - Left
the ability to plié 2 1/2" to 4 1/2"

#5 Elevé Pointe Range - Right
line from ankle to big toe's metatarsal is 90° to floor

#6 Elevé Pointe Range - Left
line from ankle to big toe's metatarsal is 90° to floor

#7 Seated Pointe Range - Right
line from ankle to big toe's metatarsal is parallel to floor

#8 Seated Pointe Range - Left
line from ankle to big toe's metatarsal is parallel to floor

#9 20 Single Leg Elevés - Right
5 counts up - 5 counts down

#10 20 Single Leg Elevés - Left
5 counts up - 5 counts down

#11 Changement - Right front
without pulling back, rolling or lifting heels

#12 Changement - Left front
without pulling back, rolling or lifting heels

#13 Single Leg Stand in Plié - Right
hold 10 counts without flicking or wobbling

#14 Single Leg Stand in Plié - Left
hold 10 counts without flicking or wobbling

#15 Degagés from 5th - Right
4 front. side and back

#16 Degagés from 5th - Left
4 front. side and back

#17 Single Leg Stand in Turnout - Right
hold 10 counts without flicking or wobbling

#18 Single Leg Stand in Turnout - Left
hold 10 counts without flicking or wobbling

#19 1 Leg elevé Retiré Parallel - Right
hold 3 counts without wobbling

#20 1 Leg elevé Retiré Parallel - Left
hold 3 counts without wobbling

#21 1 Leg elevé Retiré in Turnout - Right
hold 3 counts without wobbling

#22 1 Leg elevé Retiré in Turnout - Left
hold 3 counts without wobbling

#23 Advanced Plank - Right foot on floor
hold 10 counts without wobbling

#24 Advanced Plank - Left foot on floor
hold 10 counts without wobbling

#25 Single Leg Sauté in turnout - Right
without lifting hip or pulling back

#26 Single Leg Sauté in turnout - Left
without lifting hip or pulling back

#27 Superman with twist Right
4 counts up, 4 twist R and center, repeat L - 5x

#28 Superman with twist Left
4 counts up, 4 twist L, center, repeat R - 5x

#29 Relevé Retiré in Parallel - Right
hold 3 counts without wobbling

#30 Relevé Retiré in Parallel - Left
hold 3 counts without wobbling

#31 Relevé Retiré in Turnout - Right
hold 3 counts without wobbling

#32 Relevé Retiré in Turnout - Left
hold 3 counts without wobbling

#33 Posé Développé Devant - R and L
hold 3 counts and roll down

#34 Posé Retiré à la seconde - R and L
hold 3 counts and roll down

#35 Arabesque Combination - Right
hold 3 counts in arabesque and pirouette ending up without wobbling

#36 Arabesque Combination - Left
hold 3 counts in arabesque and pirouette ending up without wobbling

PRIMARY EVALUATIONS

Alignment and Placement

Needs Correction	Exercise	Repetitions

Feet and Ankles

Needs Correction	Exercise	Repetitions

Knees and Legs

Needs Correction	Exercise	Repetitions

Hips and Turnout

Needs Correction	Exercise	Repetitions

Core and Back

Needs Correction	Exercise	Repetitions

Balance, Pirouette and Arabesque

Needs Correction	Exercise	Repetitions

DAILY IMPROVEMENT Plans

NOTE 1: These charts were created to help you accomplish your goals by setting up guidelines from which you can work. All bodies are different. Hopefully you have learned much about yours through these studies. It is fine to substitute other exercises, which you have found work better for you or adjust the number of repetitions. The important thing is that you challenge your body to become strong or flexible enough to qualify for pointe.

NOTE 2: We all have one side which is stronger and one which is weaker. Be sure to do twice as many repetitions on the weaker side.

AS OPPOSED TO THINKING HOW SOON YOU CAN COMPLETE THESE TESTS, THINK HOW MUCH YOU CAN IMPROVE SO YOU CAN COMPLETE THESE TESTS.

ALIGNMENT AND CENTERING

If you have mastered these statements, you are ready for testing.

☐ 1. I maintain correct body alignment and hold my maximum turnout when standing on both feet.

Notes.

☐ 2. I can maintain correct body alignment and hold my maximum turnout when in elevé on both feet.

Notes.

☐ 3. I can maintain correct body alignment and hold my maximum turnout when balancing on one leg either standing or rising in elevé or relevé.

Notes.

☐ 4. In 5th center floor, I can do a grand plié and rise with erect well placed posture without wobbling or shifting my feet.

Notes.

Daily Improvement Plan - Neutral Head Placement	
ASSESSMENT #1	*Repeat exercises throughout the day and check off each set after completion in the cells below.*
Finding Neutral - Chin Carried Forward	Developing awareness of head placement for dancers who hold their chin forward. Jut your chin forward and back with resistance, then lift and lower. Stop in neutral each time. Do this until you can easily maintain neutral.
	YOUR DAILY PROGRAM: Wk. 1= 5 sets - 2x/day Wk. 2=10 sets - 2x/day
Finding Neutral - Head Inclined	Awareness of head placement. Primarily for those having difficulty maintaining their head erect when spotting. Slow walking turns with head erect during each 1/2 turn spot.
	YOUR DAILY PROGRAM: Wk. 1 = 5 sets - 2x/day Wk. 2 =10 sets - 2x/day

Note: P/I = parent's initials

WEEK 1	**MON.**	**TUES.**	**WED.**	**THURS.**	**FRI.**	**SAT.**	**P/I**
Chin Forward							
Head Inclined							
WEEK 2	**MON.**	**TUES.**	**WED.**	**THURS.**	**FRI.**	**SAT.**	**P/I**
Chin Forward							
Head Inclined							

Daily Improvement Plan - Standing Posture	
ASSESSMENT #1	*Repeat exercises throughout the day and check off each set after completion in the cells below.*
Shoulder Blade Series	Developing awareness and correction of protruding shoulder blades. 4 count Shoulder Blade Exercise and Theraband pull back and pull down exercises.
	YOUR DAILY PROGRAM: Week 1 = 10x-3x/day Week 2 = 20x- 3x/day sets
Correcting for Ribs Held Out	Corrective exercises + Correct your ribcage placement throughout every dance class and each time you think of it through the day.
Correcting for Sway Back	Core relaxed and not lifting in and up. Core exercises to strengthen + awareness throughout the day.
	YOUR DAILY PROGRAM: Increase placement awareness of ribs and core in class, especially in movements center floor and when jumping.

WEEK 1	MON.	TUES.	WED.	THURS.	FRI.	SAT.	P/I
Shoulder Blade Series and Rib Ex.							
Core Exercises							
WEEK 2	**MON.**	**TUES.**	**WED.**	**THURS.**	**FRI.**	**SAT.**	**P/I**
Shoulder Blade Series and Rib Ex.							
Core Exercises							

Daily Improvement Plan - Demi-Plié	
ASSESSMENT #2 - #4	*Repeat exercises throughout the day and check off each set after completion in the cells below.*
Positioning the Knees in Demi-Plié - #2	Knees are built to bend and straighten not go from side to side like our wrists. Rolling the knee inward is damaging to your knees. Always be aware of knee placement, and do exercises to extend your turnout found in the Hips and Turnout Chapter.
	YOUR DAILY PROGRAM: Awareness while doing all pliés in class including center floor.
Plié Depth - #3 and #4	Stretches for the gastrocnemius and soleus calf muscles. See Knees and Legs chapter. Hold 15 counts.
	YOUR DAILY PROGRAM: Week 1 = Do 3 sets/day Week 2 = Do 4 sets/day

WEEK 1	**MON.**	**TUES.**	**WED.**	**THURS.**	**FRI.**	**SAT.**	**P/I**
Core and Hips Exercises							
Gastrocnemius & Soleus Stretch							
WEEK 2	**MON.**	**TUES.**	**WED.**	**THURS.**	**FRI.**	**SAT.**	
Core and Hips Exercises							
Gastrocnemius & Soleus Stretch							

FEET AND ANKLES

Mastering these statements prepares you for testing.

☐ 1. I know and use proper weight distribution when standing on two legs, one leg or in elevé.

Notes.

☐ 2. In tendus and degagés, my heel is down as I press through the demi-pointe to a fully stretched foot with toes long.

Notes.

☐ 3. I have the ability to hold my toes straight without clenching or clawing in both elevé and pointing movements.

Notes.

☐ 4. I have strong feet and ankles that raise me up to full demi-pointe and keep me from wobbling whether on 1 or 2 legs.

Notes.

Daily Improvement Plan - Point Range	
ASSESSMENT PREP. #5 - #8	*Repeat exercises throughout the day and check off each set after completion in the cells below.*
Strengthening Your Pointe Range - #5 and #6	To extend your pointe range - do any Foot and Ankle stretching exercise in the Foot and Ankle Chapter. Hold for 20 counts. Repeating 3x = 1 set.
	YOUR DAILY PROGRAM: Week 1 = Do 3 sets/day Week 2 = Do 4 sets/day.
Strengthening Your Pointe Range - #7 and #8	To strengthen your foot muscles for demi-pointe height. Single leg elevés on a step along with 2 other foot or ankle strengthening exercises. Combine 3 exercises and repeat them all 4x = 1 set.
	YOUR DAILY PROGRAM: Week 1 = Do 3 sets/day Week 2 = Do 4 sets/day.
	BE SURE TO DO CALF STRETCHES AFTER THESE EXERCISES

WEEK 1	MON.	TUES.	WED.	THURS.	FRI.	SAT.	P/I
Pointe Stretch 3-4x/day							
Elevé on a step + 2 foot/ankle Ex.							
WEEK 2	**MON.**	**TUES.**	**WED.**	**THURS.**	**FRI.**	**SAT.**	**P/I**
Pointe Stretch 3-4x/day							
Elevé on a step + 2 foot/ankle Ex.							

Daily Improvement Plan - Foot Strengthening	
ASSESSMENT PREP. **#8 - #26 | #29 - #36**	*Repeat exercises throughout the day and check off each set after completion in the cells below.*
Building strength under the foot	Cat's Paws/Advanced Cat's Paws (Alternate feet). 4 counts. up - 4 down. Do 20x-3x/day + Doming or Caterpillar - hold up 4 counts. Do 20x-3x/day. Shown in Feet and Ankles Chapter.
	YOUR DAILY PROGRAM: Week 1 = 10x/set 3 sets/day. Week 2 = 20x /set 3 sets/day.
Strengthening the feet, ankles and calf	Seated elevés as shown in Feet and Ankles Chapter using only one foot at a time. Be sure to keep weight balanced between big and 2nd toe, elevé in 4 counts and return in 4 counts. Repeat on other foot. Do twice as many on your weakest foot.
	YOUR DAILY PROGRAM: Week 1 = 5x/set 3 sets/day. Week 2 = 10x /set 3 sets/day.
	BE SURE TO DO CALF STRETCHES AFTER THESE EXERCISES.

WEEK 1	MON.	TUES.	WED.	THURS.	FRI.	SAT.	P/I
Cat's Paws							
Seated elevé							
WEEK 2	**MON.**	**TUES.**	**WED.**	**THURS.**	**FRI.**	**SAT.**	**P/I**
Alternating Cat's Paws							
Seated elevé to Pointe							

KNEES AND LEGS

Mastering these statements prepares you for testing.

☐ 1. I know if my knees are straight, hyperextended or hypoextended and how to manage them in neutral.

Notes.

☐ 2. I open my knees out over my toes in all plié and fondue movements.

Notes.

☐ 3. I pull up through my body and hold my supporting knee straight when I do grand battement, développé or rond de jambe en l'air.

Notes.

☐ 4. I hold my hips square and don't lift or push forward with the working hip when I do grand battement, développé or rond de jambe.

Notes.

Daily Improvement Plan - 20 elevés	
ASSESSMENT PREP. #9 - #10	*Repeat exercises throughout the day and check off each set after completion in the cells below.*
Building strength under the foot	Do Doming and other foot strengthening exercises daily as previously indicated.
	YOUR DAILY PROGRAM: Week 1 = Do 10x/set - 3x/day. Week 2 = Do 10x/set - 4x/day.
	ALL elevéS ARE DONE 5 COUNTS UP AND 5 DOWN.
Strengthening the feet, ankles and calf	Double Leg elevés in parallel, turnout, and turned in for the first week. The second week do single leg only in parallel. Maintain straight knees throughout these exercises.
	YOUR DAILY PROGRAM: Week 1= Double Leg 10x for each - 3x/day. Week 2 = Single Leg elevés 20x - 3x/day.
	BE SURE TO DO CALF STRETCHES AFTER EACH EXERCISE

WEEK 1	MON.	TUES.	WED.	THURS.	FRI.	SAT.	P/I
Doming Series							
Double Leg elevės on a Step							
WEEK 2	**MON.**	**TUES.**	**WED.**	**THURS.**	**FRI.**	**SAT.**	**P/I**
Doming Series							
Single Leg elevés on a Step							

Daily Improvement Plan - Changements	
ASSESSMENT PREP. #11 - #12	*Repeat exercises throughout the day and check off each set after completion in the cells below.*
Foot, Ankle, and Calf Strengthening	Seated elevé and Seated elevé up to Pointe. Exercises from Foot and Ankle Chapter. Do one foot at a time with forearms pressing downward on thigh. Press heel up 5 counts and lower 5 counts.
	YOUR DAILY PROGRAM: Week 1: 2x/set 2 sets/day. Week 2: 3x/set 2sets/day.
	BE SURE TO DO CALF STRETCHES AFTER THESE EXERCISES.
Core Stability Muscle Strengthening	When shoulders are pulling back = Deep core stability strengthening exercises shown in Core and Back Chapter.
	YOUR DAILY PROGRAM: Week 1 = 5x/set 3 sets/day. Week 2 = 10x /set 3 sets/day.

WEEK 1	MON.	TUES.	WED.	THURS.	FRI.	SAT.	P/I
Seated elevés							
elevés on a step							
WEEK 2	**MON.**	**TUES.**	**WED.**	**THURS.**	**FRI.**	**SAT.**	**P/I**
Elevés on a step							
Foot and Ankle program							

Daily Improvement Plan - Single Leg Stand	
ASSESSMENT PREP #13 - #14	*Repeat exercises throughout the day and check off each set after completion in the cells below.*
Strengthening Feet and Ankles	Wobbling ankles = Weak feet and ankles. Do more foot and ankle strengthening exercises.
	YOUR DAILY PROGRAM: Week 1 = 10x/set 3 sets/day. Week 2 = 20x /set 3 sets/day.
	BE SURE TO DO CALF STRETCHES AFTER THESE EXERCISES.
Single Leg Stand in Plié Flicking Tendons	Single Leg Stand in front of a mirror - lift and lower your toes. Feel the muscles in your lower leg moving - not the muscles you want to use. Stand on one leg, plié pressing your weight forward and hold balance from beneath your foot. Lifting from top of foot causes the tendons to flick. Work on placement, centering and foot strengthening work.
	YOUR DAILY PROGRAM: Week 1 = HOLD 4 counts. Do 3x/day. Week 2 = HOLD 8 counts. Do 3x/day.

WEEK 1	MON.	TUES.	WED.	THURS.	FRI.	SAT.	P/I
Foot and Ankle Exercises							
Balancing in front of a mirror							
WEEK 2	**MON.**	**TUES.**	**WED.**	**THURS.**	**FRI.**	**SAT.**	**P/I**
Elevés on a step							
Foot and Ankle program							

Improving Extension	Week #1	Week #2	Week #3	Week #4	Week #5	Week #6	Week #7	Week #8	Week #9	Week #10
R Front Extension										
R Side Extension										
R Back Extension										
L Front Extension										
L Side Extension										
L Back Extension										

HIPS AND TURNOUT

Mastering these statements prepares you for testing.

☐ 1. My leg moves freely in my hip while doing degagé. My torso, arms, leg, and ankle are strongly held and centered on my stable foot.

Notes.

☐ 2. I maintain strong balancing skills when standing on one leg in plié and can hold my turnout on both legs.

Notes.

☐ 3. I can elevé center floor, in both parallel and turnout, to full demi-pointe and hold 3 counts without wobbling and lower with control.

Notes.

☐ 4. I can relevé center floor in both parallel and turnout, to full demi-pointe, hold 3 counts without wobbling and lower with control.

Notes.

Daily Improvement Plan - Degagés and Single-Leg Stand	
ASSESSMENT PREP. #15 - #18	*Repeat exercises throughout the day and check off each set after completion in the cells below.*
In 5th - Degagé Devant #15 and #16	Incorrect weight placement on supporting foot: Review alignment on one leg "Centered". Body movement/loss of balance = "TA Stability" exercises in Core and Back Chapter. Hip not free = Release your hip joint and let your joint move freely.
Degagé to 2nd	Torso leaning = Incorrect weight placement on supporting foot: Review single leg alignment.
Degagé Derrière	Degagé leg not extending straight behind shoulder = Placement awareness.
	YOUR DAILY PROGRAM: As needed.
Single Leg Stand - #17 and #18	Same as Single Leg Stand in Plié. Continue working toward being able to balance on one leg without grabbing from the top of your foot.
	YOUR DAILY PROGRAM: As needed

WEEK 1	MON.	TUES.	WED.	THURS.	FRI.	SAT.	P/I
TA Stability ex. and Clam 2 sets/ day							
Foot and Ankle work							
WEEK 2	**MON.**	**TUES.**	**WED.**	**THURS.**	**FRI.**	**SAT.**	**P/I**
TA Stability ex. and Clam 2 sets/ day							
Foot and Ankle work							

Daily Improvement Plan - Single Leg Stand in Elevé	
ASSESSMENT PREP. #19 - #22	*Repeat exercises throughout the day and check off each set after completion in the cells below.*
Single Leg elevé in Parallel #19 and #20	Body movement/loss of balance = TA Stability exercises in Core and Back Chapter. Ankle wobbling = Foot and Ankle strengthening exercises + elevés. Loosing center over balancing point = practice alignment work. Balancing = Stand in front of a mirror on one leg. Slow elevé, checking and adjusting alignment as needed. Try not to touch the wall.
	YOUR DAILY PROGRAM: Week 1 = 5x/set 2x/day Week 2 = 10x/set 3x/day.
Single Leg elevé in Turnout #21 and #22	Turnout not held in both legs. Turnout muscles need strengthening and/or to be used = Choose from "Turnout Series" exercises. Inner thigh tightness = Adductor Stretches Tension in back of the hip = Tennis Ball Release.
	YOUR DAILY PROGRAM: As needed.

WEEK 1	MON.	TUES.	WED.	THURS.	FRI.	SAT.	P/I
TA Stability + foot/ ankle Combinations							
Placement and Balancing skills							
WEEK 2	**MON.**	**TUES.**	**WED.**	**THURS.**	**FRI.**	**SAT.**	**P/I**
TA Stability + foot/ ankle Combinations							
Placement and Balancing skills							

CORE AND BACK

Mastering these statements prepares you for testing.

☐ 1. I'm able to hold an advanced plank for 10 counts and remain completely straight without wobbling.

Notes.

☐ 2. With my lower legs on a stability ball and my hands on the floor, I can do 10 pikes without falling of wobbling.

Notes.

☐ 3. I can do the twisting Superman exercise 5x on each side without taking a break.

Notes.

☐ 4. I can do the "Waiter's Bow" down to a 110 degree from a standing position.

Notes.

Daily Improvement Plan - Core Stability

ASSESSMENT PREP. #23 - #26	*Repeat exercises throughout the day and check off each set after completion in the cells below.*
Advanced Plank #23 and #24	Unable to hold a steady Plank = Do Abdominal Hollowing Lunge and Bug Legs or any other spine stability muscle strengthening exercise. Breathe normally holding the plank for 10 breaths. Make sure your plank is completely flat from finger tip to heel including head.
	YOUR DAILY PROGRAM: Week 1=10x - 2x/day Week 2 = Tilt and twist 20x - 2x/day.
Single Leg Sauté #25 and #26	When hip lifts up during a sauté, strengthen the gluteus medius = Do Clam and Side Leg Lifts 20x/set. Feet and ankles not held strongly = Start in single leg stand with plié at the barre. Elevé 2x then sauté. 4x/set Change to other leg.
	YOUR DAILY PROGRAM: Week 1 = 3 sets 2x/day Week 2 = 5 sets 2x/day Concentrate on centering and try to let go of the barre.
	BE SURE TO DO CALF STRETCHES AFTER EACH EXERCISE.

WEEK 1	MON.	TUES.	WED.	THURS.	FRI.	SAT.	P/I
Abdominal Lunge and Bug Legs							
Clam and Lying leg lifts and elevé 2x w/sauté							
WEEK 2	**MON.**	**TUES.**	**WED.**	**THURS.**	**FRI.**	**SAT.**	**P/I**
Abdominal Lunge and Bug Legs							
Clam and Lying leg lifts and elevé 2x w/sauté							

Daily Improvement Plan - Core Stability	
ASSESSMENT PREP. #27 - #28	*Repeat exercises throughout the day and check off each set after completion in the cells below.*
Superman with a Twist	Not having the strength to hold the Superman lift and do 5 twists to each side before lowering = Week I = Do Cobra, hold 5 counts, lift arms over head hold 5 counts, return to back to Cobra and lower to floor. Week 2 = Superman, twist R hold 5 counts. Then L hold 5 counts, return to center and lower to floor. This combination is 1 set.
	YOUR DAILY PROGRAM: Week 1 = 5 sets 3x/day Week 2 = 10 sets 3x/day.
Single Leg Sauté #25 and #26	Hip lifting = Strengthen the gluteus medius - Do Clam and Lying leg lifts in turnout, 20x Feet and ankles not held strongly - Do elevés w/ plié on 1 leg. Every 3rd one do a sauté.
	YOUR DAILY PROGRAM: Week 1 = 3 sets 2x/day Week 2 = 5 sets 2x/day.

WEEK 1	MON.	TUES.	WED.	THURS.	FRI.	SAT.	P/I
Cobra then lift arms up							
Clam, lying leg lifts and elevé w/ sauté							
WEEK 2	**MON.**	**TUES.**	**WED.**	**THURS.**	**FRI.**	**SAT.**	**P/I**
Cobra then lift arms up							
Clam, lying leg lifts and elevé w/ sauté							

BALANCE, PIROUETTE, AND ARABESQUE

Mastering these statements prepares you for testing.

☐ 1. When I elevé in 1st, I can rise to a full demi-pointe with maximum turnout and balance for 15 seconds.

Notes.

☐ 2. I can shift my weight and move successfully from both feet to one foot in elevé, relevé, or posé with control and balance on demi-pointe.

Notes.

☐ 3. I can stand in retiré on either leg and hold 10 counts.

Notes.

☐ 4. I can elevé in retiré, hold 3 counts and lower with control. I can relevé in retiré, hold 3 counts and lower with control.

Notes.

Daily Improvement Plan - Relevé Retiré	
ASSESSMENT PREP. #29 - #32	*Repeat exercises throughout the day and check off each set after completion in the cells below.*
Relevé Retiré in Parallel	Hip raised and body tilted = Placement work. Supporting foot not to demi-pointe = foot strengthening/stretching. Unable to balance for 3 counts = Alignment and strength. NOTE: Remember a relevé snatches the ball of the supporting foot beneath the body's axis.
	YOUR DAILY PROGRAM: Relevé retiré in parallel facing mirror. Wk 1 = 5x-3x/day Wk 2 = 5x-6x/day.
Relevé Retiré in Turnout	Hip raised/body tilted = Placement work. Supporting foot not to demi-pointe. = foot strengthening/stretching. Unable to balance for 3 counts = Alignment and leg strength.
	YOUR DAILY PROGRAM: Relevé retirés in turnout facing mirror. Wk 1 = 5x-3x/day Wk 2 = 5x-5x/day

WEEK 1	MON.	TUES.	WED.	THURS.	FRI.	SAT.	P/I
Relevé retiré in parallel facing mirror							
Relevé retiré in turnout facing mirror							
WEEK 2	**MON.**	**TUES.**	**WED.**	**THURS.**	**FRI.**	**SAT.**	**P/I**
Relevé retiré in parallel facing mirror							
Relevé retiré in turnout facing mirror							

Daily Improvement Plan - Posé	
ASSESSMENT PREP. #33 - #34	*Repeat exercises throughout the day and check off each set after completion in the cells below.*
Posé Développé devant	Posé stepped up, not sprung. Arabesque not balanced/poor placement. Supporting leg not pulled up and knee relaxed. Arabesque roll down with développé not controlled. Turnout not held. Unable to balance for 3 counts. = Posé devant with side to barre. Try releasing barre as often as possible.
	YOUR DAILY PROGRAM: Wk 1 = 5x/day Wk 2 center floor = 10x/day.
Single Leg elevé in Turnout #21 and #22	Hip raised/body tilted = Placement work needed. Not springing. Supporting foot not up to demi-pointe. = foot strengthening/ stretching. Unable to balance for 3 counts = Alignment and strength. Posés to 2nd facing the barre. Try releasing barre as often as possible.
	YOUR DAILY PROGRAM: Wk 1 = 5x/day Wk 2 center floor = 10x/day.

WEEK 1	MON.	TUES.	WED.	THURS.	FRI.	SAT.	P/I
Posé développé at the barre							
Posé to 2nd at the barre							
WEEK 2	**MON.**	**TUES.**	**WED.**	**THURS.**	**FRI.**	**SAT.**	**P/I**
Posés développé at the barre							
Posés to 2nd at the barre							

Daily Improvement Plan - Arabesque Combination	
ASSESSMENT PREP. #35 - #36	*Repeat exercises throughout the day and check off each set after completion in the cells below.*
Arabesque Part A	Unable to execute a smooth transition to arabesque = a placement and control issue. Work on centering and placement. Choose exercises from Chapter One "Alignment and Placement."
	YOUR DAILY PROGRAM: 3 exercises done 4x/side is 1 set = Wk 1 2 sets 3x/day Wk 2 3 sets 3x/day.
Arabesque Part B	Arabesque not turned out. = Placement or strength issue. Elevé in arabesque not held 3 counts. = Balance/centering issue. Arabesque leg not at 90°. = Strength issue. Roll down not controlled. = Foot and ankle strength and/or placement issue.
	YOUR DAILY PROGRAM: Relevé retirés in turnout facing mirror. Wk 1 = 5x-3x/day Wk 2 = 5x-5x/day.
Arabesque Part C	Unable to end pirouette up. = pirouette not on center. Over turning pirouette = giving too much force through arms and/or spotting.
	YOUR DAILY PROGRAM: Wk 1: Relevé retiré w/1/2 turn. Do 10x/foot. Wk 2 full turn.

WEEK 1	MON.	TUES.	WED.	THURS.	FRI.	SAT.	P/I
Part A and B Exercises above							
Part C Exercises above							
WEEK 2	**MON.**	**TUES.**	**WED.**	**THURS.**	**FRI.**	**SAT.**	**P/I**
Part A and B Exercises above							
Part C Exercises above							

Creating Your Own Exercise Program

1. CHOOSE 2 exercises or a combination of exercises which will best help you develop the skills you need to improve enough to pass a particular test.

2. Daily Exercise Chart

   a. In the top box (Skills Needed), write the skill you are working on.

   b. In the box beside it (Exercise Program to Develop Skill) write the exercise you will be doing.

   c. Repeat for the 2 boxes below with your second exercise.

NOTE: Check your book for the description of each exercise and recommended repetitions. For example - 10x 3x/day (10 times, 3 times per day).

   d. PROGRAM WEEK 1 = Write the name of each exercise and the number of repetitions you will be doing for both in these boxes.

   e. DAYS OF THE WEEK BOXES = Each time you complete 1 round of both exercises, place a check under that day ie. 3x/day = 1 check in box for each set of exercises completed that day.

   f. PROGRAM WEEK 2 = Increase the number of reps. As shown - If week 1 was hard, keep the reps the same.

   g. PROGRAM WEEK 3 = If you reach your goal, don't do this week - If you haven't, continue increasing your reps.

Skills Needed	Exercise Program to Develop Skill

WEEK 1	MON.	TUES.	WED.	THURS.	FRI.	SAT.	P/I
WEEK 2	**MON.**	**TUES.**	**WED.**	**THURS.**	**FRI.**	**SAT.**	**P/I**
WEEK 3	**MON.**	**TUES.**	**WED.**	**THURS.**	**FRI.**	**SAT.**	**P/I**

Skills Needed	Exercise Program to Develop Skill

WEEK 1	MON.	TUES.	WED.	THURS.	FRI.	SAT.	P/I

WEEK 2	MON.	TUES.	WED.	THURS.	FRI.	SAT.	P/I

WEEK 3	MON.	TUES.	WED.	THURS.	FRI.	SAT.	P/I

Skills Needed	Exercise Program to Develop Skill

WEEK 1	MON.	TUES.	WED.	THURS.	FRI.	SAT.	P/I
WEEK 2	**MON.**	**TUES.**	**WED.**	**THURS.**	**FRI.**	**SAT.**	**P/I**
WEEK 3	**MON.**	**TUES.**	**WED.**	**THURS.**	**FRI.**	**SAT.**	**P/I**

Skills Needed	Exercise Program to Develop Skill

WEEK 1	MON.	TUES.	WED.	THURS.	FRI.	SAT.	P/I
WEEK 2	**MON.**	**TUES.**	**WED.**	**THURS.**	**FRI.**	**SAT.**	**P/I**
WEEK 3	**MON.**	**TUES.**	**WED.**	**THURS.**	**FRI.**	**SAT.**	**P/I**

Skills Needed	Exercise Program to Develop Skill

WEEK 1	MON.	TUES.	WED.	THURS.	FRI.	SAT.	P/I
WEEK 2	**MON.**	**TUES.**	**WED.**	**THURS.**	**FRI.**	**SAT.**	**P/I**
WEEK 3	**MON.**	**TUES.**	**WED.**	**THURS.**	**FRI.**	**SAT.**	**P/I**

Alignment Square

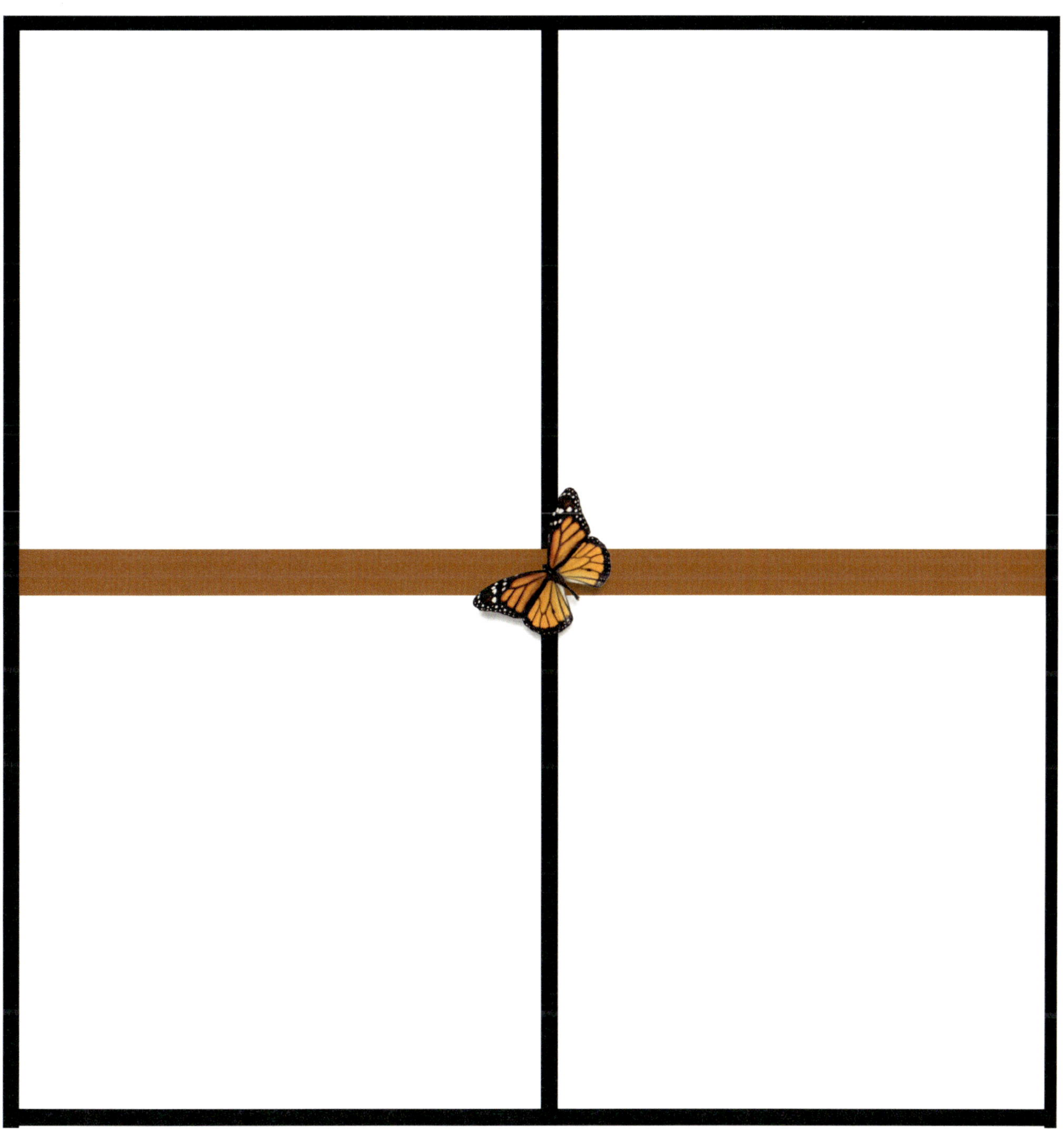

With this edge against a wall, stand in first position with the tip of your big toe on the inch mark (between 2 1/2" to 4 1/2" depending on your height) and plié to touch the wall. See page 32.

DEMI-PLIÉ DEPTH

Right Leg

one inch

two inches

three inches

four inches

four inches

three inches

two inches

one inch

DEMI-PLIÉ DEPTH

Left Leg

With this edge against a wall, stand in first position with the tip of your big toe on the inch mark (between 2 1/2" to 4 1/2" depending on your height) and plié to touch the wall. See page 32.

Made in the USA
San Bernardino, CA
05 December 2016